Married
AND WITHOUT A
HUSBAND

JUAN CLAUDIO-RODRIGUEZ

Copyright © 2021 by Juan Claudio-Rodriguez

ISBN   Softcover   978-1-953537-37-9
        Ebook   978-1-953537-38-6

All rights reserved. No part of this book may be reproduced or transmitted in any form or by any means, electronic or mechanical, including photocopying, recording, or by any information storage and retrieval system without express written permission from the author, except in the case of brief quotations embodied in critical reviews and certain other non-commercial uses permitted by copyright law.

Printed in the United States of America.

Martin and Bowman
1-855-921-1348

CONTENTS

Dedication 1
Introduction 5
Marriage 7
Her Childhood 11
The Innocent Catholic Girl 15
My Mother's Rocky Marriages 18
A New Beginning 24
The Final Straw 27
The Last Betrayal 30
Life After My Father 32
Single Parent 41
No Educational Role Model 49
Lost a Child 54
Discipline Tactics 61
The Entertainer 66
Master of Trades 73
Health Issues 76
Her Final Days 81
The News 86
The Wake 88
My Mother's Funeral 91
After the Funeral 93
Domestic Violence 97
Reference 102

DEDICATION

It is important that I write this memoir as a tribute to my mother, her life, and the struggles she suffered along it. I want to thank her for weathering the storms that threatened our security. I also want to acknowledge that I understand what she did for us as well as apologizing for adding more stress to her life. My only regret is not being able to help alleviate her suffering while she was alive. I hope that she might forgive me from the heavens above. Memories of my mother are and always will be in my thoughts. Her memories are the medicine that soothes my wounded heart. More than anything, I want to thank my mother for being part of my life and for allowing me to be part of hers.

Hold on to the Memories

When you lack courage to carry-on
because you lost a loved one,
and live in pain,
you must realize that death
is something we cannot change.

Hold on to the memories
and don't let their death
be an obstacle or interference
that stops you from being
who they would want you to be.

Hold on to the memories
and don't ever forget,
they will make you stronger
and your life you will live
in peace, without regrets.

Do not leave the past behind.
Learn to overcome obstacles
by holding on to the memories
of the one you lost
who you will never forget.

Analyze your life
and hold on to the memories
as you return to reality.
There are loved one's that need you
so, they can survive.

Do not live your life in tears
because those you hold dear
in this world no longer are.
Hold on to the memories
and they will always be near.

INTRODUCTION

People generally marry because they believe to be in love. However, marriages are formed based on certain norms, beliefs, values, and expectations. It is a legal arrangement between a man and a woman where they both have the same rights and responsibilities over all family matters including children. Sometimes, those responsibilities and expectations are not fulfilled by one or both of the partners in a marriage. Unfortunately, when one of the partners in a marriage does not fulfill the expectations and/or responsibilities of the marriage, the other partner is confronted with the decision of whether he or she should remain married. For many women neglected or mistreated in a marriage this decision can be a difficult decision to make based on their circumstances. It is up to them to decide to leave or remain in an unhealthy marriage. Unfortunately, there isn't a book that outlines the way women should be loved or treated within a marriage, help them understand their relationship with men, their behavior, and that the decisions they make impact their relationships with their partners as well as the relationships with their children.

God Loved Her

God loved her.
He gave her life
and a big heart
So, she could feel
what love is like.

God loved her so,
that he gave her children
with whom He shared her,
So, she could be loved
as God loved her.

She loved her children,
and as did God,
she sacrificed herself
and carried a burden
for the children she loved.

God so loved her,
that when He saw her suffering
He took her to where He reigns
to relieve the pain
that in her body she felt.

God so loved us,
that He descended from heaven
and our mother He took.
But, many memories He left us,
of our mother, a gift from God.

MARRIAGE

In many marriages, women are discouraged when they are emotionally disconnected from their partner. Often, in this type of relationship, many women bear the weight of the relationship and believe they are not taken seriously by their partner. It is not uncommon for women to experience feelings of abandonment due to lack of emotional support from their partner . Consequently, they carry the burden and the responsibility of making their marriage work. Therefore, it is not rare that these women feel frustrated because their marriage is unacceptable, and at the same time feel that they are invalidated and forced to assume the role of the husband. They feel as though their needs have gone unmet due to the customs and practices exercised by their partners. In such cases many women feel that they are no longer tied emotionally to their partner's because of their behavior. As a result of their emotional abandonment they often feel as though they are not heard or no longer exist in the eyes of their partner.

Our world has been formed in part due to the sacrifices made by many women. Their sacrifices have made it possible to keep our world stable and normal. In many marriages, women are willing to do whatever it takes in order to provide a safe environment for their children. Keeping the family safe and together is their priority. Many unstable marriages are threaten due to lack of support and attention due of the spouse, whose irresponsibilities threatens the safety of the children. At this point of their lives many women make decisions based on other factors despite love to justify the reason for which they remain in their marriage. It is a fact that when they arrive at this point in their relationship they have already lost their value of self-esteem. As a result, the lack of value of self has been the reason why many women put the needs of others before their own needs and have avoided accepting the fact that they have made a mistake. They fail to admit their error even though they know that their marriage was based on lies. As is, they are aware that staying in their marriage does not feel well and that they should re- evaluate their lives and their decisions in order to find true happiness. However, they do not do so because they didn't know any other way or are afraid of the uncertainty of what the future will bring them. Thus was the case of my mother. I had not realized that she lived such a life until I sat down to talk with her a few weeks before her death. Through our conversation my mother stumbled over her words and became very emotional when talking of her life. As she told me the events of her life tears began to flow out of the corners of her eyes. She wanted to stop our conversation, but I insisted that we continued. I too, let my emotions get to me as our conversation progressed. However, I held back my tears because I wanted to really know my mother and understand the things she experienced before her death.

HER CHILDHOOD

My mother was the third of 14 siblings. She grew up on a farm surrounded by valleys and hills filled with beautiful green grass, lakes and rivers. Around the house extended the fields of my grandfather's farm that filled the air with the freshness of the giant mountain which increased in grade each time even more the further away from the house. A cool breeze could be felt against one's skin as it descended from the mountains. On the farm it appeared that one could almost touch the clouds, while standing on one of the mountain tops, and feel the warmth of the sun as it gently caressed the body. It was truly an oasis of tranquility where the animals sang in harmony while they roamed the farm joyously.

Every morning she woke up to the singing of the roosters, clucking of chickens, and the mooing of the cows. These wonderful farm animals provided the family with eggs and fresh rich milk which they enjoyed with their coffee, coffee that my grandfather harvested, roasted and milled. The aroma of their freshly roasted coffee itself was something to talk about. There was hardly a need to go to the city. My grandfather harvested all kinds of fruits on the farm. There was every fruit that you could imagine: oranges, tangerines, grapefruits, bananas, raspberries, papayas, mangoes, mamey, guanabanas, acerolas and many others. He also cultivated tobacco, yams, malangas, tomatoes and many other food products. My grandfather harvested these crops and sold them to stores in the city, where the city folks would purchase the various crops produced by the farmers like my grandfather. Living on the farm was as though you were living in another world where all your needs where met. It was on the farm where my mother spent her childhood during a simpler, more innocent and happier time. It was the place where she would play and enjoy her childhood. Moreover, it was an extraordinary place where family and friends gathered to enjoy nature, eat, and interact with each other. The breathtaking beauty of the surrounding nature was magical and incredible. It was no surprise to see those who visited the family stunned with its splendor. At night the sun landed on the farm as it slowly descended from the sky. It would disappear into the land, and as it vanished it took the light of day, covering the farm with a dark velvet blanket. When there wasn't a glimpse of daylight on the farm, the coqui's could be heard throughout the night singing their song with the hope of finding its mate. Local legend state that the coqui sings in order to give his loved one a way to find their way back to them. The sound heard at night seemed as if all the animals that came out gathered around the farm to accompany the coquí. Together, under the light provided by the fireflies,they sang a beautiful ballad that filled the night with peace and harmony. Crickets chirped, owls hooted, frogs croaked and the buzzing of the mosquitoes brought all of their beautiful sounds together in perfect harmony. The noises of the night were mesmerizing and a joy to hear. The pleasant sound of the night animals was enough to make anyone fall asleep. Life on the farm was quite contrary to the life in the city. Normally, the city was bombarded with the sounds of cars passing by, construction workers working, and the loud music coming out of many homes were a constant distraction. It was on this peaceful farm that my mother grew into a lovely young lady without any struggles.

Your Palm Trees

Puerto Rico beloved Island,
your shores and meadows
are full of palm trees,
whose beauty inspire me
and bring peace to my life.

The smell of your palm trees
perfumes my body
and covers me with love,
as the bud of a flower,
it soothes my soul when it blossoms.

The fresh sea breezes
whistles a beautiful song.
As it passes through your palm trees,
It reminds me of my homeland
and touches my heart.

The freshness of your palm trees
feeds comfort to the sore spirit
and serves as a home for birds,
where they can take a break
from their flights and make nests.

My dying wish is to be buried
in your soils which have given me
the breezes of your beautiful palm trees
that have kissed my forehead
and grazed my soul.

Your palm trees are in my heart.
They have served as an inspiration.
Your mountains they filled with beauty.
My body they have fanned and caressed
and my thoughts they have seized.

THE INNOCENT CATHOLIC GIRL

My mother was raised in a strict catholic family. Every night she met with the rest of the family in the living room to pray. My grandfather always led the prayer at the end of the day before going to bed, and at 5:00 in the morning, every morning, to give thanks to God for all the blessings he had bestowed upon the family. The family prayer service normally lasted between an hour and a half to two hours. Every Sunday morning the family went to church. They did everything together.

My mother was not an educated woman. Though, she was formally educated only up to 6th grade, which today would be an equivalent to ninth or 10th grade, she was a very sophisticated woman. What my mother lacked in education she made up for in heart, desire and loyalty. With the passing of the years my mother matured and while in school she met a young man with whom she fell madly in love. My mother was fifteen years of age when she fell in love with the young man and started dating him. The young man was a year older than her. He was very good looking and popular with the girls. They dated on and off for a period of two years. During that time the relationship with the young man began poorly and never improved. During the first two years of their relationship my mother had dissolved the relationship nine to ten times due to his cheating ways. However, he would use his charms and good looks to get her to date him again. Regardless of having experienced being cheated on numerous times previously she would give into his pleas every time. She would do so because he would always promise that he would not cheat on her again. A promise that he never kept nor did he intend to keep while he was courting her. Nonetheless, she always forgave him because as she simply put it, she was in love. He was her first love and she was willing to do anything for him. One evening while sitting at home, shortly after her seventeenth birthday, she had stepped outside the house to use the latrine (out house) and never made it back to the house that night. The young man with whom she had fallen in love was waiting for her outside. As she exited the house she met him in an embrace and together they left the farm and eloped. She willingly gave up the life she had on the farm for a future of uncertainty. This young man turned out to be my father.

Wandering Eyes

Your wandering eyes
undress the infidelity you try to hide.
When you look at everyone within your sight,
my world begins to slowly die,
as you forget that I'm by your side,
an act, you know is not right.

As your eyes wander
with a passion that your emotions excite
your heart tends to forget
all your illicit gestures
and the pain my soul endures
as you hurt me with your lies.

When I see your eyes wander
my heart begins to ponder
when did you begin to doubt
If I was enough for you,
if I am still your muse,
or if your love for me is true.

MY MOTHER'S ROCKY MARRIAGES

A few months after my mother and father eloped they were married. Throughout their marriage they had seven children. The first child was born a week after my mother turned eighteen years of age. Regardless of my mother's current condition my father continued having extramarital affairs. Marriage, her love for him, or the fact that he was about to become a father did not stop him. No one could stop him, whom had wandering eyes, from having affairs. Throughout my mother's first pregnancy he had several affairs. The fact that she knew with certainty that he was cheating was not enough for her to leave him. However, my mother believed that my father would stop being unfaithful to her once they had a child. My mother was completely blinded by the love she felt for my father and hoped for the impossible from him. My father never stopped having romantic relationships with other women despite her pleas and efforts during their thirty-three years of marriage. Throughout his marriage to my mother, he did not show any concern for my mother or their seven children because he never stopped being unfaithful. My mother was heartbroken throughout their marriage. However, she hid her true feelings because she did not want their children to know what was happening. She did everything within her power to prevent them from knowing the truth. My father was not as considerate, he did the opposite. He never made any effort to prevent their children from knowing that he was going out with other women. Although, there were rumors about the extramarital affairs of my father, my mother pretended to be ignorant of the facts and continued sharing her life with him. She tolerated a lot from him during their marriage. Many women would have not tolerated his behavior, but not my mother. She remained in a marriage whose relationship was based on lies and lack of consideration for one another. When my mother was twenty-four years of age she had already conceived five children. I am the fifth child to be born. I was born a month after she turned twenty-three years old and her marital situation did not improve regardless of the fact that she now had five children. My father had not changed. Her life was filled with dissapointments, and for now, although divorce was against her religious beliefs, she was already thinking about the possibility of divorcing my father. However, the thought of giving their children a stepfather was something that she didn't want to do. In her mind, the thought of finding another man worthy of her childrens heart was non-existent. She thought there wasn't a man in the world whom would be willing to raise her five children as his own and loved them as they deserved. She was merely a naïve twenty-three years of age woman with five children, whom were all nearly a year apart from each other. By now she had lost her faith and trust in men. Nonetheless, it took my mother a long time to realize that my father had stripped her of her innocence and dignity. The lack of commitment of my father with her and their children threatened the relationship and safety of their children. To him his family was not of importance because he was more interested in satisfying his carnal desires. He was more concerned with feeling the thrill, excitement and emotions he felt when he had intimate relationships with other women. His lack of concern for my mother and their children coupled with his constant involvement in extramarital affairs were hurting his marriage and his relationship with their children. He completely disrespected my mother and our family. His actions clearly made her feel as though she did not exist. Even worse, he made her feel as if she was invisible regardless of all her efforts of trying to keep their marriage together. Moreover, trying to keep their family together. He no longer saw her as the person he once loved and wanted to spend his life with. My father did not care whether or not his actions inflicted pain on my mother or his children. His total disregard and contempt for his family was obvious as he went around in public with these women. To make matters worse, he also arrived home late at night on several occasions with his shirt stained with lipstick and a scent of cheap women perfume. As is, he never apologized for his actions, nor did he show any remorse for the pain he had inflicted on my mother and their children. I recall how my mother would always argue with him as she became aware of the facts. They would argue about the findings for a few minutes, and then go to bed together. In an attempt to avoid making a scandal in front of the children and to keep my father's extramarital affairs and their feuds over his behavior away from their children my mother would argue with my father in their bedroom. It wasn't until I was 8 or 9 that I came to a realization of the turbulent relationship she had with my father and of all the skeletons she was hiding in the closet. She never put herself first which always lead to them remaining together. Instead, she would turn a blind eye in order to keep the family together. It was as though she considered it worthless of the effort to try to make him change. It was her choice to make and she never thought of life without my father. Meanwhile, my father had forgotten about the feeling he felt when he first started dating my mother and of the feelings that motivated him into eloping and marrying her. He continued his cheating ways throughout their entire marriage and when I was born he left to Chicago to work . He eventually started his own business leaving my mother and his five children behind in Puerto Rico. When I turned 6 months old, my mother left me behind to live with my grandparents when she was informed that my father was living with another woman in Chicago and did not intend to send for us. So, she picked up her belongings and my four siblings and went to Chicago to confront my father. Five years later, they came back to Puerto Rico for me and together we all returned to Chicago where we lived until 1975. To my surprise, I had one more sibling whom I had not met and to whom I was nearly three years older. While we were living together in Chicago as a family my youngest brother was born in 1972. Three years after my youngest sibling was born we all returned to Puerto Rico. A few months after we arrived to Puerto Rico my older brother was struck by a bicycle as he was walking home from church. He passed away on December 8, 1975 due to head injuries incurred during the accident. My mother remained in Puerto Rico until she divorced my father. When my mother divorced my father, most of us (my siblings and I) had already left home to start our own lives. My two younger siblings were the only one's that remained at my parents home with my mother.

Invisible

I am invisible
and it makes me agonize
knowing that you don't see me
when I'm by your side,
that you don't hear me
though in your ear I shout,
that you don't feel me
when I caress your body.

I am invisible.
It has me terrified
knowing that you have no clue
that I am disappearing
like footprints in the sand.
Your love for me is skewed
and you cannot see me.
It's what you choose to do.

When the idea of love is askew
and you look right through me
as if I weren't there
it's made me realize
how I am slowly fading
although I am in plain sight
because you just don't care
to make things right.

My heart is blue.
We are strangers.
You know it is true.
I am invisible
regardless of what I do.
You just can't see me
or the love I feel for you.
It's what you chose to do.

A NEW BEGINNING

My mother had tolerated my father's infidelities for more than 30 years. She had grown accustomed to his ways and tolerated it as long as she had children living at home. She even accepted the fact, that he was parading his mistresses and taking them out to different places in the surrounding area. Something that my father never took time out to do with her . Though, he never took time out to do any of those things with my my mother, she always seemed to turn the other cheek when it came to my father's extramarital affairs . However, I do remember the time when my father had the audacity to parade his mistress in front of us while we were playing in the park. The fact that he was parading his mistress in front of us and our friends while we were playing in the park really angered my mother and made her lose her patience and want to change her situation. She took control of her feelings and decided that she would no longer let my father humiliate her. That day, it so happened that my mother had come to the park to watch us play when she saw my father drive right past us with his mistress in the car. She immediately ran to the street and blocked the path of the car by placing herself in front of the car. Her spontaneous reaction forced my father to stop the vehicle. As the vehicle came to a complete stop my mother ran to the passenger door and pulled my father's mistress out of the car. She dragged her by the hair onto the street. We all ran toward them and got between my father and my mother. Now, I don't ever recall hearing my mother curse with the exception of that day. My mother called his mistress all kinds of names that I'd rather not write about and told her that she had no scruples. She went on telling her that she had no shame because she was known to have ruined other marriages. To our dismay, our father remained in the vehicle while my mother had her way with his mistress. It took all of us to separate my mother from my father's mistress.

A New Beginning.

A new beginning is an opportunity
where we discard the failures
that we could not escape
and tried to forget.
We must separate them
from the things of the past
that hurts our heart
and fills us with emotions
if new relations
you want to achieve.

We must forget everything bad
and not hold any grudge
in order to forgive
and our mistakes rectify
if you want a new beginning,
which arouse's feelings of love
that arise from pain
and changes our life.

Starting again
lifts the soul and heart
of those who want to improve
and a new life start.

THE FINAL STRAW

The final straw that got my mother to leave my father was when he moved in with one of his mistresses. It just so happened to be the mistress my mother dragged out of the car by the hair. Normally, it didn't matter whether he had his affairs as long as he would make it home. The fact that he didn't return home for several days and that he had no intentiton on returning must have angered my mother even more than usual, because she took all of his belongings, packed them, and put them in front of the house for him to collect. Was it the fact that he chose his mistress over his family that angered my mother the way it did, or that he completely abandoned us and did not return? Whatever it was, he was no longer welcomed in our home. Shortly after the encounter in the park my mother gathered enough courage and self-respect that she filed for divorce. The divorce was finalized a few months later. In the beginning of their divorce she saw herself as a victim and would cry herself to sleep every night. As time went on she stopped seeing herself as a victim. She no longer wanted to make the pain she felt over the divorce determine her future. While they were divorced my father made several attempts to rekindle their relationship, but my mother did not want anything to do with him. She was finally liberated from the person that had ruined her life. All the love she felt for him could no longer serve as a shield that hid the facts that he had eyes that wandered upon seeing other women, whom he pursued and had affairs with. Her love for him no longer hid the facts that he did not really love her as he claimed. She had finally realized that he had stolen her youth and her innocence by condemning her to a life full of disappointment. Moreover, she had realized that life continued without him and that she was strong enough to keep it together in order to move forward with confidence and optimism. She had finally put herself first, set her priorities straight and committed to changing her lifestyle. She was no longer going to be the doormat my father would step all over. No one wants to see their parents divorce each other, however, it was a welcomed change. We all viewed their divorce as an opportunity for our mother to grow and find the happiness that she once felt but had lost. She even started to believe that she could be happy and live her life without our father.

Fearless

I am no longer a slave to fear.
I will not wonder where to hide
because I am terrified of my worries
and have my dreams swept away.
I refuse to be afraid or pushed around.
I will always stand my ground.
In the darkness or in the light
I am prepared to fight.
God has made everything right.
He has blessed me with his armor,
my enemies he has crushed,
and embraced me with his love.
From fear he has set me free.
Thanks to God I will not shed any tears
because he has conquered all of my fears.
Now, I can fulfill my greatest desire
and walk straight into the fire.
I will no longer drown in fear.
It will not paralyze me,
or control my life
by drowning me into madness.
It will not destroy my reality
because with God I am prepared to fight,
living unafraid and free.

THE LAST BETRAYAL

Life after my parents divorce was a challenge for my mother. Though she managed the family finances she had never imagined how difficult it would be to survive after the divorce. She never planned her future without my father or considered the financial support he provided. Nonetheless, being divorced was quite liberating because she was no longer in a cruel and miserable marriage. She had finally put an end to a bitter marriage. A marriage to which she was tied to for so many years because of the children and the money my father brought home. Fortunately, she regained her identity through her independence and was committed to being happy. She was no longer in a relationship where she was constantly being belittled and disrespected and she was not going to allow her marital experience with my father determine her future. In the beginning, she lacked confidence. She doubted that she could rebuild her life due to the financial difficulties she was faced with after the marriage. However, she was lucky to have supportive children who helped her get over the financial difficulties.

I Will Rise

When hope was gone
and anguish filled my soul,
in your arms weakened I cried.
You gave me hope
with words of wisdom
that raised my spirit high.
You made it clear
when you comforted me
to have faith and keep in mind,
that people will soon see
the lies that were rooted
which brought me pain
will soon be left behind.
you said it would not come as a surprise
when through it all I will rise,
that the reason for my demise
will no longer me terrorize.
I saw the honesty in your eyes,
and heard the truth you had spoken
in the words you said that were nice
that kept me from my demise
and promised that through it all I will rise.

You reminded me not to lose faith
Through it all, from the beginning,
That God's promises are not lies,
That if I am not defeated
I am still winning,
and through it all I will rise.

LIFE AFTER MY FATHER

My mother remained single for nearly two years. During that time she was approached by the handy man whom we had known for many years. She hired him to do some repairs at her house. He too had been married and was recently divorced. The fact that they were both recently divorced made it easier for him to slowly labor his way through to her heart. A few months after being together they were married. He was everything my father was not. He would do all the necessary things from electrical, plumbing, carpentry and all the essential things required to keep your house working and looking the way it should. Most importantly, he was always affectionate toward my mother. In the beginning of their marriage everything was perfect. She was living the life she always imagined. She was finally in a relationship where she was appreciated and loved by the man she married. However, as time went on her dreams were slowly being shattered again by another person she trusted and married. Her new husband's true personality came out to light. He started to be controlling, manipulative, and condescending. He drank alcohol everyday and as he drank, he would complain about my two younger siblings who were still living at home. At the time they were 17 and 22 years of age. He would argue with my mother in the hope of getting them out of the house. This all began just a few months after they married. My mother would not give in to his demands and told him that her children weren't going anywhere. As a result of my mother not caving to his demands he drank with every passing day even more. One evening after playing softball at the park my younger brother went home. It was late and everyone was already in bed. He walked in the house and turned the dining room lights on. As he sat down to eat a snack at the dining room table prior to going to bed, my mother's husband walked out of the master bedroom and turned the dining room lights off while my brother was eating . When Carlos (my brother) got up and turned them back on, my mother's husband would turn them off again. This went on three or four times. When my mother's husband turned them off the last time it made my brother lose his patience and he started arguing with him. When Carlos got to the point that he was about to hit him for being inconsiderate, my other sibling and my mother, who were in their rooms sleeping, both ran out to the dining room to find Carlos and my mother's husband arguing. Luckily, they got to them before it escalated from being a verbal argument to a physical fight. They helped difuse the argument by keeping them apart. By now, my brother Carlos was so frustrated that he stormed out of the house and went back to the park to cool off. A few minutes after my younger brother left the house, my mother and my brother Rafael confronted my mother's husband . They questioned his reasons for doing what he did. He apparently didn't like that he was being questioned, because, he began arguing with my brother and mother. Unfortunately, my brother Rafael was not as nice as my younger brother. He did not appreciate that he was arguing with him or my mother. Rafael did not like my mother's husband attitude, or how he handled the situation with my younger brother. Well, he made things worse by arguing with my brother Rafael, because he was already angry at the fact that he was awaken because of the unnecessary commotion. Unfortunately, for my mother's husband, he should have not started an argument with my mother and my brother Rafael. Because this angered my brother even more that he too lost his patience and started punching my mother's husband so fast that he could not defend himself. During the onset of fists, my brother landed a fist or two on him that literally broke his nose to the point that he needed immediate medical attention. Within 10 minutes after storming out of the house, my younger brother Carlos received the news that he had to go home because my other brother had beaten up my mother's husband. Upon returning to the house, he saw that my mother's husband was bleeding and his first thought was that he regretted thae fact that it was not him who beat up my mother's husband. He was still angry and wanted to beat him up. He was truly disappointed that it wasn't him who had inflicted the injuries on my mother's husband.. The night after the beating while my mother and her husband were alone at the house he began to argue with my mother about the incident the night before. He got so angry with my mother that he stabbed her in the chest during the argument. After he stabbed her, he took off through the wooded area in back of the house, leaving my mother on the floor for dead. When my mother noticed that he had left, she got up while pressing down on her chest to stop the bleeding. She gathered enough strength to go across the street to get help from the neighbors. They immediately went to the park where my brother Carlos was watching the local softball teams play. When the neighbor got to my brother he informed him of what had just transpired. Upon hearing the news he immediately ran to the house to check on our mother. When he arrived to the house, he and a friend, who was with him when he got the news, put my mother in his friend's car and took her to the hospital which was 30 minutes from our house. His friend drove as fast as he could to the hospital through the curvy roads of San Lorenzo, Puerto Rico. A bad decision, such as taking a curve too fast or too wide could have been the reason for which they would have all ended down the side of one of the several dangerous ridges along the way. They were fortunate enough to make it to the hospital without any further incidents. Had they not made it to the hospital as quick as they did my mother would have bled out in the car and passed away. As is, my mother barely survived the vicious attack. Her husband missed puncturing her heart by a centimeter. She was hospitalized for a few days while she recovered from the attack. While she was hospitalized the police caught up with my mother's husband and arrested him. He had been hiding at his daughter's house. During the sentencing process my mother went to see him in jail. Once again, my mother was blinded by the love she felt for her husband that she was willing to do whatever he asked. My mother went as far as asking my wife, who was in Puerto Rico, while I was stationed overseas, to take her to every court appearance he had so that she could talk with the state attorney. In all of the court appearances he had my mother plead for lieneancy on his behalf. Somehow, her husband convinced her that he stabbed her out of love. He said that he stabbed her because he couldn't stand seeing my brothers take advantage of her. He also claimed that he was high on drugs and alcohol and did not realize what he was doing because he had never done drugs before. He said that the only reason he used drugs was because he was very angry with my brothers and blamed them for his actions. She believed everything he said and forgave him. After several meetings with the state attorney my mother managed to convince him to reduce her husband's sentence. He served less than two years in jail and once he was released my mother took him in her house as though nothing had happened. My younger siblings were still living at home when he was released from jail. She pleaded with my brothers not to start a fight or give him a reason to argue with them. She reminded them that he was her husband and that they all had to get along while they lived under the same roof. My relatives and friends of the family were dumbfounded with my mother's actions. They could not believe that she took him in again. Everyone advised her not to take him back because he could not be trusted. However, she just wouldn't listen and went against their advice. From that day on my mother's husband no longer argued with my mother in front of my brothers. Nor did he argue with my siblings. Whenever he had a problem with them he would get drunk. He drank every night and every night he complained to my mother of my siblings. To avoid the gossip and the looks of everyone in the city, who talked about her, my mother sold her house and moved to Florida. Together they moved to West Palm Beach, where they lived for a period of eight years. By now, both of my younger siblings had married and were living in their own homes.

    I left the United States Army in 1996 and came to live in Florida. I stayed with my mother temporarily until I was able to purchase a home in Port Saint Lucie. I lived with my mother for a period no longer than two months. During that time my daughter was five years old and my son was 8 months old. During our stay at my mother's home, her husband complained constantly. He did not complain to me, instead he would always make his complaints known to my mother, and she would then inform me of his complaints. She would also beg me to not say anything because she didn't want him to be angry with her. He complained that he had to smell my son's dirty diapers that were thrown in the trash and that he had to listen to the noise that my children made. My mother's husband complained the entire time. To avoid creating problems for my mother and having a confrontation with her husband I went to live with my sister and sent my wife and children to Puerto Rico for a few months while I looked for a house to buy. A few months after having gone to live with my sister I bought a house and began attending the University in Florida. Meanwhile, my wife was working at a salon as a cosmetologist. In order to lessen the financial burdens incurred by my studies, my wife had to work . My mother also helped make it easier for me to study and for my wife to work by looking after our children. She cared for them at her home. One day, she approached me in tears and told me that she could not baby sit my children anymore because her husband had forbidden her from babysitting them again.. When I heard that he forbid my mother to take care of her grandchildren, my children, it angered me greatly. Until now, I had not said a word to him because my mother had asked me to not say anything. However, I had enough of my mother's husband's nonsense. I was so angry that I asked my mother why she would allow her husband to forbid her from caring for her grandchildren. She told me that she had no choice. I was stunned after hearing her response. I couldn't believe that she was choosing that piece of shit over her family. Just the thought that she chose him and cast us aside like trash made the feelings of abandonment I felt as a child emerge again. This time, it was because my mother was casting aside my children. She had chosen a man instead of her family, her blood, as she did with me when I was little. I was so upset by her comments that I told her that I was I angry and disappointed by the fact that she allowed her husband to forbid her from babysitting her grandchildren.

As I was expressing my feelings to my mother, I happened to look in the direction of the kitchen where my mother's husband was standing listening to our conversation. He realized that I had seen him and immediately began running when he noticed that I was going toward him aggressively calling him all sorts of names. As I was approaching him, and he was almost within my grasp, he locked himself inside his room. I banged on the door while yelling at him to come out and tell me like a man what he had told my mother. He remained in the room hiding like the coward he was. My mother finally caught up with me and pleaded with me to leave him alone. I just looked at her and told her not to worry about it, that if she was choosing him, that she could have him. I told her that my children and I were no longer coming to her house, or wanted anything to do with them again. We did not see or talk to her again for nearly 18 months. Needless to say, my children were growing up without seeing their grandmother because of her inability and unwillingness to stand up for herself, nonetheless, for her grandchildren. Eventually, my sister approached my wife and told her that my mother was ill and that it was bothering her that we had not seen her for such a long time. It took my wife several weeks to convince me to go see her. Though we had mended our relationship it was never the same from that point on. It was distant. Most people that knew me would say that I may have been cold and unaffectionate toward her. As is, we barely spoke to each other. When we first started talking again I mentioned to my mother and my wife that if my mother's husband said anything, regardless of how miniscule it may be, about my children again that I would give him a beating he would never forget. For years he would stay clear of me and did not address me. But, as time went on little by little he began talking to me. During that time I kept my conversations with him to a minimum. I only expressed to him what I needed to and nothing else. I made it a point to never hide my feelings from him, which angered him. He never told me anything about what he felt. However, he was going behind my back speaking ill of me to my mother and brother Rafael who lived with them at the time. His feeling toward me did not concern me at all, and it did not surprise me that he never apologized for his actions. At least he was smart enough to keep his distance from me and reserved his comments.

Toward the end of their marriage, my mother had decided to separate from him because he too had been unfaithful to her like my father, her first husband had done. Her husband's affair with the other woman did not last long, and as previous occasions, he blamed us for his actions. He claimed that my mother had become distant because of us and as a result he found someone who paid attention to his needs. My mother, being the kind-hearted person that she was forgave him and took him in as she had done before. They remained together for approximately 4 -5 more years. However, his constant drinking, his bickering and his continuous attempts to distance her from her children were the reasons my mother ended their marriage.

Your Betrayal

How sad the agony,
you have left in my heart
that has shattered my soul.
Because of your betrayal
everything has changed.

You say it was not your intention,
That you did not mean to hurt me
and that you lost your mind.
Now, I know you never loved me,
because you cast me aside.

Enough lies and empty promises
as they have broken my heart.
What we had has no solution.
Today my heart is filled with anger
and does not know forgiveness.

Even if you return repentant
there will not be another occasion
where I forgive you.
I have erased you from my life
and never mentioned you again.

Deep scars you have left
embedded within my heart.
I prefer the solitude,
than to submit to your cruelty
and be a victim of your betrayal.

It is difficult to forgive.
The past doesn't matter.
You did not know to value,
the love that I gave you
which you betrayed and shattered.

SINGLE PARENT

My mother faced many challenges while married to my father. Despite the fact that they were married for more than 33 years to each other and lived under the same roof, she carried the burden and stresses of a single parent. My father was never around to negotiate or discuss the day to day responsibilities as the head of the household. In fact, my father's lack of interest in the family and constant absence placed upon my mother the responsibilities of a sole parent. My father held her accountable of raising their children alone. She had the freedom to do what needed to be accomplished without consulting my father. It must have been a tedious endeavor for my mother to tackle, because every time she took charge of a situation, or made decisions on behalf of the family that required a prompt response, my father would always argue with her. He would criticize her for not informing him and then complained of the expenditures that took place. Regardless of whether my mother discussed or failed to discuss any financial decision with my father, any attempt she made to talk to him about the budget would be deflected by him getting angry. In his eyes he always believed that any expenditure was a waste of money and an unnecessary thing to do. Although, it may have been empowering for my mother to do things without consulting my father, she was always reminded by him of the fact that he was the bread winner of the family; the one and only who provided the financial means for every decision made and every accomplishment of the family. Their relationship was contentious and exhausting not just for my mother, but for us children as well. We were constantly told by our father that the only thing we were good for was for eating and spending his money. As is, our father never bonded with us or showed us any affection. He never modeled good character or cared about being a good role model for us. My father never took time to teach us the skills needed to be successful or how to tackle the day to day challenges of life. Morover, he failed to teach us how to thrive on our own. Basically, he never fulfilled his responsibilities as our father, and because of this, we never learned from him how to ride a bike, how to catch a ball, play any sport or anything related to education. All the things that a father should teach his children we had to learn on our own. My mother was also absent to these types of activities. However, in her defense, she herself did not know how to ride a bicycle or how to play any sport. The irony was that my father always took credit for our actions when one of us would do something well in school or in sports although he had nothing to do with how we turned out to be academically or athletically. I remember several occasions when my father would address some of my siblings as dummies or bums because they received a D or an F in school. I also recall several occasions where he would take credit for or boast about me getting straight A's. This was one of the very few times that he actually said something positive about the family and would boast with pride by saying, "that's my son." As if he had done anything to help me achieve such accomplishments. He would also fill his ego as he boasted when one of us would do well in sports which we were playing without his approval. Still, he was always set in his ways and because of that he never wanted us to experience anything that brought excitement to us, like sports. He would always say that we didn't need to participate in sports. But, thanks to my mother we were able to practice and play sports. She would always let us participate in sports without his approval as long as we made it home prior to my father coming home from work. Whenever he would find out that we were engaging in some sort of physical activity such as sport he would tell her that if we were hurt while participating in a any sport or extracurricular activity that he would hold her responsible. If we weren't home because we were at the park and it was getting close to the time in which my father would be arriving home, my mother would always walk up to the street corner to call out our names and remind us that we needed to get home in order to avoid getting into a dispute with my father over our involvement in sports. Though it was embarrassing for us, being able to enjoy life playing with other children was worth the embarrassment. It was definitely a sacrifice that I was willing to make in order to live a normal life for a while.

As a kid, I stood out in basketball, soccer and baseball. I played in organized team sports and when we had to travel to play another team, my mother would let us go without my father's approval. She always begged us to make it back to the house before our father got home. If we needed money to pay for any fee or to cover some of the travel expenses incurred she would take it from my father the night prior without his knowledge. Whenever we were late getting home, he would always chastise us and complain about how we were spending his money.

When it came to birthday parties, Christmas gifts and going on vacations we were not as fortunate as most children. We never had our birthday celebrated which after a while became quite upsetting. Instead, our mother would ask our father for money to give to us. For our birthday, he would give us two dollars and for Christmas he would give us five dollar. My father never gave us the money himself. He would give the money to our mother to give to us. However, in the process of doing so he would always complain. He was always loud enough for us to hear his complaints. I know, it doesn't sound like much, but for someone who rarely got any gifts, two dollars was a fortune, and it was worth having to put up with my father's comments. I remember, thinking of the ways I would spend it, and it would depress me even more because I never seemed to have enough money to get anything I really wanted. Instead, I used the two dollars to buy candies and enjoy the moment without complaining.

My father never did anything for my mother that made her feel loved. AS is, I don't remember my father ever buying any flowers for my mother for her birthday, Valentine's Day or their anniversary. However, he did lavish all of his mistresses with gifts and took them out on extravagant dates. He never considered any of the expenses he incurred to lavish his mistresses with gifts or dates an unnecessary expense. He was so blatantly disrespectful and inconsiderate that one evening my uncle (my mother's brother) and my father nearly got into a fight because my father took his mistress to a restaurant where my uncle was having dinner. When my uncle saw them walk into the restaurant, he told my father that he had to take his whore out of the restaurant . He told him that he didn't want to see them together in any place where he was. My father avoided the confrontation as he quickly turned around and left the restaurant with his mistress in his arms.

Taking a trip or just spending quality time as a family during a vacation was something that we never experienced as well. My father never made an effort to spend quality time with us or to take us anywhere. He would always say that we couldn't go anywhere because he had to work long hours on a daily basis to support us. My mother never learned to drive a vehicle, so she relied on our father to take us wherever we needed to go. Nonetheless, it was my mother who would take time to make the arrangements to take us to the river. If lucky, she would coordinate with one of her brothers to take us to the beach. Going on a scheduled vacation as a family was not something we were blessed with. Had it not been for my mother's creativity and spontaneous thinking, we would not have been able to do anything or go anywhere.

Selfish as it may sound, the fact that my mother did not discuss every piece of information, or divulge results of conversation we had with her, with my father was quite liberating. It eliminated some of the pain of dealing with my father's negativity and abuse. Now that I am an adult I believe that I grew up in a toxic environment that was filled with conflicts and arguments on a daily basis. Especially after my father would come home intoxicated. To prevent us from being impacted by my father's drunkenness and irrational behavior my mother would always ensure that we were all in bed prior to his arrival to the house because she feared for our safety. Regardless of the time my father arrived to the house, my mother would have to get out of bed to cook my father dinner. He refused to eat left over food or eat food that was made earlier in the day. It could be two o'clock in the morning, my mother would have to get up from the bed in order to cook him dinner. Then, she would have to stay awake with him to accompany him while he ate. Once he finished eating, my father would go to bed, and my mother would have to remain in the kitchen cleaning the kitchen by herself.

My father was always abusive when he was intoxicated. He was also more susceptible to become angry over money or annoyed with my mother over how she was raising us to be bums whom constantly mooched on him like parasites. My mother always knew how to tune him out. She was very good at difusing any arguments by ignoring him despite his intimidating and condescending behavior. She was very brave and innovative in many ways. She employed nocturnal tactics in order to get money. She would always wait for my father to be asleep while she remained in the living room watching television or in the kitchen cleaning prior to going into their master bedroom. While in the bedroom she would maneuver around the room with the skill of a Ninja in search for his wallet. Then, once she found it, she would take money out of my father's wallet. She would only take money from him to buy supplies, food that was needed in the house, or to give to us when we needed money for sports or school activities. My mother did some serious juggling in order to keep us well-fed and well-dressed. My father would always count his money prior to going to bed in front of her to let her know that he knew the exact amount of money he had prior to going to bed. Every morning without fail he would recount his money. Usually after he recounted his money, he would approach my mother and accuse her of taking money. He would complain about the missing money and assure her that he did not lose it, and that she must have taken it. My mother would always tell him that he must have miscounted the money the night before because he was "a little intoxicated " as she lightly put it. Upon hearing this he would mumble some profanity and then leave for the day.

You Will Miss Me

You will miss me
when I am gone,
and I am no longer by your side.
You will miss
with whom you shared your thoughts,
and your secrets you would confide.

You will miss
the way I smile
everytime we reconcile,
the way we shared our bed,
the way I look at you
and read you like a book.

You will miss
the way I caress your body
and in my arms you slept,
the way you I would awake
and a kiss from you I take.

You will miss
the way we fought
and the best of each we sought
because you were always in my thoughts.

You will miss
the way I always said,
that I love you
every night and every day,
and how happy it made you feel.

You will miss
the way it was
when nothing mattered
but you and me.

You will miss me
can't you see
how your life will be
if you are not a part of me.

NO EDUCATIONAL ROLE MODEL.

Neither of my parents were good role models when it came to educating their children. My father went as far as telling me when I was a child that he did not have any money for me to go to college that I was responsible for paying my way through college. The only parental involvement to help us through our academic years came from my mother. Although, she never learned English, she made us sit in front of the television to watch Sesame Street, Mr. Roger's Play House and other educational programs. The television was our first teacher and it was through television that we learned English, the alphabet, basic math and reading skills that helped us through our early childhood development. Though my mother was not educated past the sixth grade, she always encouraged us to stay in school and to develop healthy habits that would enable us to succeed and achieve our dreams. However, when we were older, one of my youngest siblings skipped school 76 days in one semester and my parents did nothing about it other than beating him. They were ignorant of the fact that he had been skipping school because they never checked on our progress with the school . As is, they never checked with the school to see if they could do anything to help us improve or to ensure that we fulfilled the school attendance requirements. Nonetheless, other than beating my brother they never held my brother accountable for his actions or took it upon themselves to be more diligent on checking on his progress. He eventually dropped out of school while in the third grade at the young age of 15. He was held back in third grade four times. When asked, he would always say jokingly that he was held back because the teacher was in love with him and not because of his continuous absence and disregard for authority. We were not fortunate enough to have parents who would help us go through the series of developmental stages that are important to the development of our intellectual, emotional and social skills. It was their choice to have kids, but it was also their responsibility to guide us and to teach us how to make wise decisions in life that impacted our future. It seemed as though it never crossed their mind that they were failing to prepare us for life and for the future. I'm no expert on parenting, and I know that I have made mistakes and that there is no right or wrong way to parent. However, I believe that when we have children, we have the moral responsibility of providing them with the basic needs such as food, clothing and shelter without making it an issue or complaining about it. Furthermore, I believe that as parents we owe it to our children to help them succeed in this world which they did not ask to be in. It may be a crazy and chaotic world but we owe it to them to prepare them for it, and not contribute to making it a worse place for them to be in. Our responsibilities should not end when they turn eighteen years old or when they emancipate themselves from our homes. We should want to help them succeed. I know that my goal in life, for my children, was to ensure that they attended college and obtained a degree. I often told them while they were in high school that they had no choice but to attend school . I instilled in them the desire to attend college through encouragement and example. As children they knew that they were going to college and that their only responsibility was to get good grades. I often reminded them that they didn't have to work while in high school or college because their mother and I would always provide them with what they needed. In fact, I would always tell them that I wanted to see them achieve more than what I have achieved in my lifetime. My motivating factor for raising my children the way my wife and I raised them was that I did not want to be like my parents. I often used my parent's lack of parenting skills as an example of what not to do and to better my own parenting skills. I know times were different when I was growing up and that my parents were not highly educated but, the fact remains that they brought us into this world, and they should have at least instilled in us the desire to succed. Had it not been for my mother who did what little she could do for us I cannot imagine the dreadful life I would be living.

Misery

Misery you keep me company,
though you can't be seen
everyone notices you with me.
You hold me captive
and won' t let me go.

You have shown your power
As you filled my heart
With misery and sorrow
And everlasting pain
That Darkens my soul.

You suck life out of me
and fill me with fear,
an everlasting feeling
that brings me to tears
Whenever you are near.

My world you turn upside down
and make me frown
as you Follow me all around.
I try to hide from you
but, I am always found.

I would like to forget you.
However, I know I can't
Because of my emotions
I am fully drained
Whereas, nothing remains.

Now Disappointment and resentment
In my heart only remains.
Misery, when you are with me
I don't think of my pain
Because I am no longer sane.

you fill me with sorrow
and deprive me from joy.
You have seized my thoughts,
and destroyed my dreams
by condemning me to a life of suffering.

My heart is weak and weary
and my soul is darken
with solace and sympathy.
Misery, If I am to survive
In my life you can no longer thrive.

Misery, you have tormented me
and never passed me by
I must let you go in order to survive
or my life will end
in a tragedy tomorrow.

LOST A CHILD

As a parent, I believe that the most devastating thing that could happen to a parent is the loss of a child. Parents are not supposed to outlive their children. But, on December 8, 1975 my parents had to deal with the loss of my oldest brother. He was 15 years old at the time. His death was rather unexpected and unfortunate. On his way home from church he was struck by a bicycle. As a result of him being struck by the bicycle he fell to the ground and hit his head on a rock. He had suffered a head injury that put him in a coma. After being in coma for nearly two months and having undergone several surgeries, doctors determined that my brother was brain dead and that there was nothing they could do to help him recover from his fatal wound. It was at that time that my parents were confronted with making the decision of letting my brother go. Their pain was noticeable to everyone. However, they made the decision to let him go, and of having the machine that kept him alive unplugged. Minutes after the machine was unplugged, my brother passed away. My mother had forever grieved my brother's death. As the days after his death turned into weeks, and the weeks turned into months, and the months turned into years my mother's grief did not fall short of devastating. However, she did not give into her grief, nor did it become a paralyzing grief to which she would succumb to. Time did not become the healing factor that would stop her from grieving. Instead, she had become at ease with her grief and did not let her sorrow stop her from living her life because she realized that she had other children for whom she had to live for. It has been more than four decades since my brother passed away. Yet, my mother still gets emotional over it. She still feels the pain of having lost her child and gets sad as she thinks of him. However, now she has learned to live with his loss and mainly gets emotional on days such as his birthday or the anniversary of his death. I am certain that she still grieves his death on a daily basis. Nonetheless, the difference now is that she has learned to keep her emotions inside and mainly displays them on special occasions.

My father's lack of concern for us was something he never hid from us. However, when my brother passed away, it was the first time that I remember him display any affection toward us. He had always shown favoritism toward my tow oldest siblings, my sister and my brother who passed away. My brother was the second child born and I believe that he and my oldest sister were the only ones he really wanted. As for the rest of us, it was obvious to us that we were a burden to him. We were nothing else but an added expense, which he made clear with his belittling comments and the fact that he stated several times that he wished he never had us. However, the evening my brother passed away my father broke down in tears. Upon seeing my father in tears several thoughts crossed my mind immediately. How could a man who was so abusive to us show any emotion toward my brother. As I contemplated the situation I was quickly drawn to the fact that he had always shown his favoritism toward my oldest brother and my sister. His lack of concern for the rest of us and his favoritism toward them was obvious when it came to punishing us. He would always beat every one of my siblings to include myself with the exceptions of his favorites. He held the rest of us accountable for every mistake made, no matter who made it, and physically beat all of us with his fists for the actions or misbehavior of any one of us. Today, nearly forty years later, I still recall the last time my father approached me with anger in an attempt to beat me for something I was not guilty of or had any control over. I was fifteen years old. There were only three siblings remaining at home, myself and two younger siblings. I was attending high school and my siblings were in elementary school. My brother to whom I am nearly three years his elder, had gotten into trouble in school. He was caught vandalizing the principal's office at the elementary school he attended. When the news got to my father he was so angry that upon his arrival to our home he came straight toward me to hit me because of my brother's actions. I tried to reason with him. I tried to make him understand that I could not stop my brother from doing what he did because I was at a different school thirty minutes away. It did not matter to him. He was the judge and the jury in our home. He had already sentenced me to his beating prior to coming home and nothing was going to stop him from carrying his sentence out. When he came to hit me, I took a stand for myself, putting my fists up. I told him that if he wanted to beat me that he would have to fight me. He was shocked. My mother just stood there totally baffled without saying a word. My father thought about what I had said and replied, "so you think you are a man". I looked at him straight in the eyes and told him yes. I told him that I was tired of getting beat for something I had no control over or part of. My mother continued to remain silent. Perhaps, she was in fear for her safety as well. The fact that I stood up to him must have crushed his world. It was becoming evident to him that he could no longer control us through fear and intimidation. I could only imagine that he thought that he was losing control of us. His authority over us was being challenged and the firm fist in which he ruled over the family was finally loosening. He could no longer oppress us by beating us. As for me, I was in shock. I finally mastered enough courage to stand up to the man who ruled my world with an iron fist. The same man who impose on me numerous unjustified and unmerited beatings. The man we all grew up fearing more than what we respected him. It infuriated my father to see me stand up to him that he walked toward his bedroom where he had a shot gun. On the way toward his bedroom all I could hear was him saying, "so, you think you are a man. Well, I am going to treat you like a man." He went on making threats, saying he had something for me. I knew what he was referring to and I immediately ran out of the house. It was nearly three in the morning when I finally decided to return to the house. On my way home I had made up my mind that I was going to leave my parents home and go to Florida to live. I figured that I had relatives in Florida with whom I could stay. I realized that if I stayed in my parents' home I would have to put up with the abuse, and maybe end up getting badly hurt or killed. When I returned to the house my father had already fallen asleep and my mother was out on the porch waiting for me the whole time. She was crying and worried about me. She told me that I didn't have anything to worry about that she had spoken to my father and settled him down. I looked into her eyes and told her that I was not staying home much longer because I planned on going to Florida to live. She thought that I was crazy and asked me how I was planning on going to Florida without money. I told her that I had been saving money for over a year. At the time I was working as the official score keeper for all games in the park where we lived, and I also worked at the milk dairy near our house. I asked her to contact my relatives and ask them if I could stay with them. She contacted an uncle of mine and he said that he would look after me. At no time did my parents try to stop me nor, did my father ever apologize. I understood that my mother had been grieving over the loss of my brother, and now that I was leaving her home under the circumstances at hand that her silence was a sign of despair beccause I was leaving home as a result of my father's behavior. However, I felt as though they were both pleased that I was leaving. I often wondered if they would even miss me. Two months after the encounter with my father I left my parents' home in Puerto Rico and went to Florida. When I got to Florida I went to school and worked full time. Prior to graduating from High School I enlisted in the Army. I served the military for nearly fifteen years. I remained in the service up to the point when President Clinton reduced the armed forces, and I was offered to get out of the service under a medical pension.

Eight years had passed since I left my parents home before I decided to go back. Unforthunately, my sole reason for returning to Puerto Rico was to see my grandmother, whom was critically ill and in her deathbed, before she passed away and to say my farewell to her at the funeral. My grandmother passed away and with her death I lost the woman I first grew to know and love as my mother. My grandmother loved me unselfishly and she did not judge or chastise me. She taught me how to walk and speak. But, it was my mother who taught me the basic core values that has made me who I am today.

Death

Death is not a choice.
But, something we must face.
It comes to everyone
regardless of their age.
It is not a book
where you can turn the page
and correct the mistakes
that in life you made.
Death numbs the body
for an eternity.
It takes your soul
and sets it free.
Death does not put
the world on hold,
nor does it wait on anyone
to grow sick or old.
Through death
walls are closed
and everything fades.
It leaves behind only memories
of who we used to be
and puts tears in the eyes
of loved ones left behind.

Death is a fate
we cannot escape.
I hope you remember
to keep me in your heart
and not fill it with rage.
Death comes to everyone
regardless of age.

DISCIPLINE TACTICS

Our mother raised us to be good human beings with decent values and she encouraged positive behavior through discipline. Sometimes, her methods of disciplining us were a little harsh and unfair and even caused harm to us that will be with us throughout our life. Both of my parents believed in spanking, which was really more like beating, as their method of choice to discipline us. To them addressing bad behavior occurred whether we were out in public, or in the privacy of our home. Embarrassing or humiliating us in public did not matter to my parents. Regardless as to where we were, they were always willing to impose corporal punishment in order to prevent future problems. Sometimes, I felt that my parents beat us not to encourage proper discipline but out of frustration. I believe, that beating their children was their mean of letting their frustration out and the severity of the beating in which they beat us was not only immoral but also illegal. It has come to mind, now that I am an adult that I can fully comprehend my parents marriage. My father's aggression was merely his way of letting us know that we were to blame for his being married to my mother. I don't doubt that he felt trapped in a marriage which he could not escape from due to the number of childrens he had to support. The way in which my mother beat us was less aggresseive than my father. She too let her frustration determine the severity of the beatings she gave us. Although she never said anything, I believe that the frustration she felt was imposed onto her by my father's behavior and lack of interest toward the family. Most of all, I believe that it was a direct result of my father's inability to show her lhat he loved her. Nonetheless, I believe the beatings they gave us were sometimes violent, excesive, aggressive and unreasonable. In many cases, the beatings imposed by my parents were criminal acts that merited getting arrested.

My Fathers' beating were unfair. Especially, when he placed unreasonable expectations on us. For example, holding us accountable for the behavior of our siblings. I can honestly say that most of the beatings I ever received by my parents were not because of my doing. On numerous occasions throughout my childhood I was beaten by my father because of the actions of my younger siblings. They would pick fights with me and when I would retaliate I would be the one getting beat by my father or mother for hitting my younger siblings. Unfortunately, I would suffer the same consequence when my brother, who is a year older, and I woud fight. They favored him and did not hold him as accountable because according to my mother he was sick. My brother was born with a sunken chest and a webbed hand. He had an inferiority complex growing up and always felt that he had to do better than me. Unfortunately, for him, I would always beat him at every sport and everytime we played each other we would end up in a fight. I believe that he intentionally started fights with me in a final attempt to at least beat me at something. Nonethless, it too was a lost cause. I would always beat him. My parents would in turn beat me because I should have not fought with him knowing that he had a disability. Getting punished by father was humiliating and demoralizing. He would physically beat us with his hands, sometimes they were opened and other times they were closed. His beatings did not stop after one or two hits, he literally beat us until he got all of his frustration and anger out of his system. If he was drunk,, his punishment bared no limits. He got carried away and extended his violence from physical to mental by exposing us to verbal abuse. He would chip away at our self-estem by telling us that we were worthless and that we would not have a future, at least one where we would be successful.

The only difference between my fathers beatings and my mother's was that her beatings were always physical and not phsycological. She did not toy with our emotions by telling us that we were worthless. My mother beat us with whatever was at arms reach. She whipped us with belts, tree branches, sticks, and even with an extension cord. I was the one at the receiving end when she used the extension cord. She whipped me so many times with it that particular day. It was excruciating. She had branded me like an animal, I still have the scar on my thigh. Whenever, there wasn't anything near for her to whip us with, she would take off her chancletas (sandals) and beat us with them. If we ran from her in an attempt to avoid being beaten she would throw her chancleta at us. She never missed us. She whould always hit her target no matter how far we were from her, even if we had turned a corner to avoid being hit. Somehow, in her hand the chancleta functioned like a boomerang. It maneuvered around the corners, hit us and even knocked us down. While we were down my oldest sister, my mothers' favorite, would run after us like a hunting dog and grab us by the hair. She would then take us to my mom like a hunting dog would return the prey to its master, so that my mother could impose her beating upon us. I recall getting away from my sister's hold on several occasions. To make matters worse, once loose I would strike her out of anger. All that did was infuriate my parents even more and get me a beating that was even worse. Had I known better, I would have had them all arrested.

After a while I learned to cope with these beatings. Nowadays, I have used my childhood negative experiences to strengthen my relationship with my own children. I know we all make mistakes, but how many same mistakes can a person make before they learn from it? Well, I used my parents mistakes to learn what not to do and how to strengthen my capacity for empathy. I have made it a point to always let my children know that I love them and that they are the most important things in my life. I am not saying that I haven't made any mistakes or that I am the perfect parent. I too, have made mistakes and at times when I did make them I saw myself as my parents. At that moment, I realized that I allowed my parents to unconsciously influence the way I disciplined my children. I exposed my children to the same type of discipline I received by my parents, but not as severe. A discipline that manifested in violence. I have made every effort to avoid making the same mistake twice. My past has been an experience that I have tried so hard to erase. Thus, I am completely against and resist being dominated by frustration. I have learned to manage my emotions and to organize my thoughts before reacting to any situation. In controlling my emotions I have learned to resolve conflicts in a less violent way.

Use Your Voice

Use your voice
To take a stand
and make demands
for someone to hear you
and lend you a hand
to fight oppression
across the land.

Use your voice
and you'll be heard,
as you let people know
what has you disturbed,
and to always protest
what you detest.

Use your voice
When you have fallen apart
Because the one you love
has stolen your heart
since the beginning
right from the start.

Use your voice
and soon you will see
the changes you thought
you could not achieve
will become a reality
and you'll succeed.

THE ENTERTAINER

My mother was quite an entertainer. She enjoyed having company over and would always go out on the limb to entertain them. She would never hesitate to coordinate with our family social events where we could gather to spend some quality time with each other. She would coordinate events where we would play Bingo and have supper. Playing Bingo was something she loved to do with the family. She enjoyed their company but, playing Bingo excited her the most. Whenever, she sat down to play Bingo she would play 3 to 4 cards at a time. It normally took her a little longer than most of us to play them, but the challenge of doing so was a delight for her. Sometimes, in order to avoid having the game delayed more than usual we would help her play her cards. At times, had it not been for us who would tell her that she had won, she would have missed out on the opportunity of collecting the prize. The excitement of winning for her was a delight to see. She would scream out, "Bingo" and immediately reach out for her prize and drag it across the table to where she sat. Then she would sort of hug her prize, to conceal her winnings in a childish way. She could spend the entire night playing Bingo, especially if she was winning. Now that my mother has passed on playing Bingo will definitely not be the same without her. I will no longer hear her scream "Bingo" or see her facial expressions of happiness that filled the room with joy everytime she would win.

My mother was quite a cook. Whenever we had company over, which was often, she would cook up a feast. Everyone loved her food. Food was an essential part of her life and cooking for others was the source that excited her the most. I believe that she saw herself through food. It was as though she received the love and acceptance she sought from my father through cooking food for everyone who loved her food. To my mother food was not just a source of nourishment, it was also a source of communication where she could express herself to the fullest. It opened doors of communication with other wives and relatives. Whenever we had company over it was not unusual for family members and friends to go to her to vent about their problems. She would be the light in peoples lives especially when they were down and living their darkest moments. She always knew to say the right thing that would put smiles on their faces regardless of what their problem was. However, she never vented back about her own rocky relationship. My mother was always willing to sacrifice herself in order to help others. However, she was not willing to have others help her when it came to her personal relationship. In doing so, my mother remained silent and kept her problems to herself. She never sought help for thee emotional storms in which she found herself. My mother was an expert at hiding her emotions from everyone. At the same time, those who knew of my fathers' escapades with other women never told my mother. Nonetheless, though she always knew when he was having an affair, she was always the last to know who he was having the affair with.

I recall many family gatherings where my mother would be the main attraction. I believe she was the main attraction due to the food she cooked. People always asked for her recipes and compared her dishes with dishes cooked in fine restaurants. Though I have had some pretty good meals in my life, it was the Christmas holidays meals that my mother cooked that would always make my mouth water the most.

Whenever our family got together during the holidays at our home or at the home of one of our family members my aunts would come early to our house, or the house where we gathered to help my mother make pasteles (meat pies similar to a tamales) or morcillas (blood sausages) .

During our family gatherings normally all of the wives would gather around the kitchen table and talk about everything that had taken place since the last time they saw each other. Everyone did something to contribute to putting the food together. While the women were busy in the kitchen cooking the splendid meals, the men were busy playing dominoes in the living room. They were always downing some beers or liquor while playing dominoes. The aroma of the food kept everyone wondering when dinner would be served. To keep the men happy my mother would always make alcapurrias and fried morcillas as appetizers. She would have one of us take the appetizers to them where they were playing dominoes. I always loved being chosen to take it to them because I would take a piece of the fried morcillas from the plate I was delivering and eat it before I got to them. By the time the food was ready everyone would be starving. When it was finally time to eat all of the adults were called to the dining room table, which was literally covered with the holiday feast.

The presentation of the food was always picture perfect. It was an image that could have been the cover of a cook book. First, my mother served the traditional arroz con gandules which was cooked to perfection. The pork in it would crumble to pieces upon being touched by a fork. The rice was perfectly cooked and accompanied by a delicious pastel, potato salad, guineo en escabeche and roast pork, which was tender, moist and filled with flavor. The skin of the pork was crispy and scrumptious. Everything was perfectly placed on the plate and looked so succulent. When everyone was finished eating, an hour or so later, everyone but my father would compliment my mother and the other ladies that helped her cook for the amazingly satisfying meal they prepared. When dinner was finally over my mother would start cleaning dishes while my aunts would help clear the tables and put the leftovers in containers. My mother always cooked a large amount of food because prior to leaving everyone would take a plate of food with them.

It is no wonder how my mother's cooking helped my father's business flourish. Every weekend she prepared special dishes which my father sold at his bar. People would come from nearby towns on the weekends just to purchase the food my mother had prepared. She would make cuchifrito, mondongo, sancocho, alcapurrias, empanadas and other dishes. The people that frecuented my father's bar, and the people that came from nearby towns to buy my mothers food loved her cooking so much that on numerous occasions the food my mother prepared for my father's business would run out shortly after she had cooked it. My father always forbade my mother and us from going to his bar. She was only allowed to go to his bar prior to him opening it for the purpose of cleaning or cooking the meals in the kitchen area my father had built in the back of the bar. As teenagers he would get angry at us regardless if we tried to stop by to get a soda or a bottle of water. However, we were allowed to go to the bar during the week only for the purpose of delivering the food my mother prepared for him for dinner, and on the weekends when we were forced to go just for the sole purpose of cleaning up the place.

Although my mother's life was not picture perfect she had a great outlook on life that was infectious and lifted peoples spirits. When something bad happened my mother would always entertain us in order to make the best out of the worst situations. She would look at the situation with a positive outlook, find something good out of it and go from there. If nothing good could be said, she did not mind making fun of herself in order to get us to laugh. She would make facial gestures, flip us a birdie, stick out her tongue or she would say something really funny in order to get us to laugh. At times she would breakdown into this ridiculous dance that she did that would make everyone forget what had angered or annoyed us. Her gestures and dances would always make us laugh and become the center of the conversation. My mother gave people hope. Her highly spirited soul took the darkest moments in people's lives and lit them bright as she filled their lives with joy.

I Will be the Light

I will be the light
that eliminates the stress
and helps you stand your ground
to confront the problems
that brings you down
when your life is a mess.

When life's struggles
obscures your views
and things go wrong
regardless of what you do
I will be the light
that guides you through.

I will be the light
that gives you comfort
when every door
is closed in your face
and you feel trapped
in a place without escape.

I will give you hope
by extending a hand
that will lighten your load
and give you a reason
in your sea of darkness
to carry on.

I will be the light
that keeps you sane
when the emotions you feel
fills you with pain
by lighting your path
to a better day.

When you call on me
I will shine bright
to help you see
and lend you a hand
to help you fight
for what you stand.

I will be the light
that helps you survive
and gives you a reason
for which to thrive
by making you believe
there's nothing you can't achieve.

MASTER OF TRADES

An expert of trades my mother was not. However, due to my father's absence she had to learn some carpentry and plumbing. There was always an enormous amount of repairs that needed to be done in our home. In several circumstances these repairs turned out to be far more stressful for my mother than she imagined they would be. My mother never realized how much work had to be done or that it required certain skills in order to fix something. She just believed that if she could repair whatever was damaged that she wouldn't have to hear my father complain about how much money he would have to spend to fix the issues. Whenever, there was a leaking pipe in the house, she would make an attempt to repair it. She would spend hours under the kitchen sink attempting to repair the pipe. If she was unable to do so, then and only then she would tell my father. My father's complaints and criticism would always slow the progress of a repair because he would get angry, which fostered resentment, rising tension and emotional withdrawal. He would complain as always because in addition to having to spend his money on our family, he knew nothing about anything and because of that he would have to pay someone to do the repairs. My father was lost when it came to doing any repair in plumbing, carpentry, electricity or automotive . He did not possess any skills other than knowing how to seduce women. If there was carpentry to be done my mother would be the first to grab a hammer and a pair of pliers to do the repair. They may have not been the appropriate tools for the job at times but, somehow she would find a way of making use of them to accomplish the repair. If something needed to be built, she was the one who gathered the materials and built it. She built all of the cages where we raised rabbits, chickens and parakeets. Sometimes, they did not serve the purpose she intended because they were inadequately built. The cages sometimes failed to keep the animals secured inside of them. I recall one time when she had put chickens in a cage she had just built in the morning to find out later that same morning that they were running loose in our yard. We would then have to chase after the animals, secure them as best as we could until she made modifications to the cages that prevented them from escaping again. If the house needed painting, it was my mother and all of the children who would paint it. If concrete needed to be laid down around the house, my mother would mix the bags of cement and lay it with her bare hands. My mother would do all of these types of chores and more without my father's knowledge. Normally my mother would do the repairs with the money that she had taken from my father while he was asleep and saved for when the need arose. She would save the money so she wouldn't have to hear him complain when asked for money to do the things that needed to be done.

Relentless

I will not give up
When sorrow fills my heart,
Hope is gone,
empty promises remain,
or my trust in people
will never be the same.

I will not give up
when people tell me
I don't stand a chance,
or my efforts are useless
that I should not take a stand.

I will not give up
regardless of what they say,
or the mistakes I make
because, they make me try harder
to overcome what is in my way.

I will never give up.
I will fight to the end to seal my fate.
I will exhaust every avenue
until I have no energy left.
Even then, I will pick myself up
and I will try again, until the end.

HEALTH ISSUES

My mother had several health issues that I believe stemmed from her personal life. Illnesses that were the results of her life being in shambles . Basically, they were the results of the dissatisfaction and disillusionment she felt throughout her marriages which slowly and gradually disintegrated her personality. My mother was literally hounded by the illnesses that lead her to death and made it impossible for her to live a normal life.

Doctor's diagnosed my mother with diabetes in her early thirties. A disease that makes no distinction for race, ethnicity, gender or age. Her diabetes eventually caused other complications such as high cholesterol and high blood pressure. Due to the improper management of these illnesses my mother was the victim of several heart attacks and kidney failure. The fact that she did not follow a proper diet coupled with her lack of a daily exercise routine made it much harder for her to gain control of the disease as she got older.

My mother's unhealthy lifestyle did not enable her to control her blood sugar level. She was constantly upset and disappointed with the men in her life, and her depression did not help her stabilize her blood sugar level because it was influenced by her emotional state of mind. To make matters worse my mother also smoked for more than sixty years which also had a negative impact on her blood glucose, cholesterol and blood pressure. Together these conditions made it a lot more difficult for her to control a sinister disease like diabetes. As a result of her unhealthy habits, my mother was in and out of the hospitals because of theses medical conditions. She was admitted into the emergency room dozens of times. On several occasions, we were told by the attending doctors that our mother was not going to survive and the suggested that we say our final good byes to our mother. Yet, on every occasion she managed to beat the odds and leave the hospital with minor complications.

At the age of 77 my mother was diagnosed with terminal cancer. The cancer was so advanced that it had already damaged her kidney, lungs, esophagus and thyroid. When the doctor diagnosed her with cancer it was the darkest moment of her life. They doctor told us that our mother had 2 to 4 months to live. It was horrifying and heartbreaking at the same time. Nothing in this world could prepare us for this devastating diagnosis. Fear and panic flooded my every thought. It was exhausting but, a reality that we all had to face. There was nothing we could do at this point. The only thing that was left for us to do was to prepare for the outcome of the demoralizing news we had just received. It felt as though we were struck with a brick on the head. Everything about it was unsettling. It seemed like we were living a dream which rapidly turned into a nightmare. The news of our mother having cancer had stricken everyone in the family. I didn't have time to filter the news because it was too much to bare. To avoid worrying my mother about the diagnosis I had to be strong; and not let my emotions overtake me or make me break-down into tears. I looked away, took in a deep breath and put up an invisible barrier to conceal my emotions from her. At the end of the day I had to consider my mother first, the pain she was enduring, and the kind of life she was now living. Though, I didn't want to lose my mother, it no longer could be about my own needs. It had to be about the needs of my mother who was dealing with a terminal illness.

It must have been extremely upsetting for my mother to know that there was nothing she could do about her terminal cancer. She was put into a heart shattering situation where the only thing she could do was to continue living her remaining life as normal as possible, knowing that she was awaiting certain inevitable death. To be aware of that every day of her life, if you could call living in excruciating pain every minute of the day, must have been horrifying and depressing. However, she had a wonderful support system of family and friends that made it easier for her to keep on going through life as normal as possible although her life line was slowly decaying.

Death was knocking on her door as it did on previous occasions. My mother had a massive open-heart surgery and struggled to recover from it, and her continuous battle with her heart problems and diabetes which kept her in and out of the hospital the last two years of her life. However, her desire to live and not leave us behind enabled her to defeat death on these previous occasions. Unfortunately, this time was different. Death was knocking hard on her door and refused to leave regardless of her screaming, kicking and franctic tantrums. Death at was staring hard at her. It was looking at her square in the eye. Death could no longer be denied. She had terminal cancer, a sinister disease we all had to face together. The ugly truth was that death had come for our mother and all of us had to accept the fact that death was a natural order of things.

Knowing that my mother was diagnosed with a terminal disease was a physical and emotional toll that weighted down heavily on all of us. We were faced with the uncertainty about what the future held for all of us. We had to embrace the fact that our mother would not be with us much longer. In addition, we had to consider our younger sibling who lived with our mother. He had been on dialysis for more than three years and his medical condition made it impossible for him to work. They were both on disability benefits which they used to help pay for their rent, utilities and food. How would he be able to survive without the financial support my mother provided him? While my mother was in the hospital she asked us to look after him. We all promised her that we would look after our brother and reassured her that he was in good hands.

Prior to our mother's passing her attending doctor told us that her body was too weak to handle radiation or surgery. Though, cancer may have been the cause for her death, my mother had been slowly dying years prior to her being diagnosed with cancer. Nonetheless, I believe her death was accelerated the day she was told that she had cancer. The fact that she was told surgery and chemotherapy were not an option to help her survive the disease weakened her spirit even more. But, in my eyes, her personal life was the main reason for her death. The disappointment and desilusionment she felt throughout her marriages had affected her so negatively that she fell into a strong, long term depression that eventually weakened her body causing it to develop diabetes, a high level of cholesterol and high blood pressure. All of these factors together sucked the spirit and will to live out of my mother's body. Cancer was just the nail that sealed her coffin.

Fading Away

Lord I pray today
you give me strength
in my heart and thoughts
as I watch my mother fade away
fighting a battle
she cannot win.
Memories of my mother,
full of life and joy,
changed to sadness and fear
as her body weakened
and death grew near.
My heart began to race
as I quickly realized,
she was slowly dying,
tears ran down my face
and I couldn't stop crying.
So, I began to pray
to god whom I implored,
cease my mother's suffering
So, she's no longer sore.
Take her to heaven
and welcome her home
where she won't be alone
as you put her to rest.
Nothing will be the same
without her presence here
to inspire my spirits delight
and give me a reason
to live and fight.

HER FINAL DAYS

During our mother's final days doctors advised us that she had to be placed into a hospice facility. However, we decided to keep our mother at home, where she could be surrounded by loved ones throughout the day. We were all against placing her in a unfamiliar environment like a community disability center . Our decision was based solely on the fact that there are so many patients living in these disability centers who are cast out of society and are dealing with the drama of being abandoned by their children. Our purpose of treating our mother at home was so that she could die with dignity as she battled a terrible and incurable illness. We were against placing her in a center where her basic physical needs would be addressed but her emotions might be disregarded because of lack of compassion by her assigned caretakers. We wanted to give her the opportunity to live the rest of her life as normal as possible surrounded by the people she loved and who loved her.

Our mother was transferred from the hospital to my sister's home where she would live her last days. While she was there she was assigned two hospice nurses. In the beginning they came to my sister's house to care for our mother 2 to 3 times a day. As the cancer progressed the nurses were assigned to care for my mother every minute of the day. Each nurse worked a 12 hour shift up to the minute of my mother's death. The nurses assigned to my mother were carefully and diligently monitoring her and would inform us of her status as her symptoms progressed. They did everything within their power to make our mother comfortable. They administered my mother's medication, and with the assistance of my sisters, they would bathe her, and would place her on her side or back to relieve the pain and agony her body endured as the cancer progressed . As she was approaching her final moments, she laid in bed with her mouth wide opened, tongue hardened due to dehydration and breathing was shallow. To make her feel better we would swab her mouth with a wet sponge. She wore a CPAP machine that sent oxygen into her lungs to help her breathe. She also had plastic tubing pumping medicine into her body to ease her pain. Seeing her in this condition, struggling to breathe, fighting to inhale enough oxygen to keep her alive, made me wish that God would stop her suffering and take her to her resting place, her final destination. Her suffering was long and difficult for everyone, especially for my oldest sister who spent every minute of the day with my mother. She did everything she could to ensure my mother did not suffer throughout her battle with cancer. She was at my mother's beckon call whenever she needed her. As my mother got closer and closer to death, and her struggle to survive became harder, made it even more obvious that my mother was suffering. Though my mother never complained during her battle with cancer, it became harder for everyone to see her suffering the way she did. I believe that to ease her suffering we all prayed to God, at one point or another, asking Him to end her suffering and take our mother to heaven with Him.

 As the cancer was spreading and her internal organs were failing, I felt as though life was in fast forward and death was approaching rapidly. Regardless of our attempts to slow things down a bit, I was hit once again with the hard facts that there was nothing we could do to stop this. Watching my mother die was the worst experience I had ever endured. However, our wonderful support of family and friends that made it easier for us to keep going as our mother's body slowly decayed and she lived out her last moments.

Having watched my mother, whom I love, suffer the way she was suffering, gave me a greater sense of gratitude and admiration for her . I thought of her present battle and of all her previous battles in life she endured. I also thought of all of the sacrifices she made for us. I stroked her hair as I was lost in the thoughts of all the things she did for us. I kissed her cheek as I told her that I loved her and that I did not have any grudges toward her. As I told her how I truly felt, I saw her eyes fill with tears which slowly rolled out of the corner of her eyes. It was at that moment, though she did not say a word, that I believe she finally realized that I did love her and that regardless of whatever happened between us in the past, I had finally come around. She understood that I appreciated her sacrifices and loved her for whom she was, my mother.

My father, who had been married to my mother for more than thirty years, came to my sister's house with his new wife to see my mother while she was in hospice care at home. They walked into her room where she was lying in bed to share a moment with my mother. My siblings were in the room while my father and his wife greeted my mother and gave her their blessing. Immediately after they greeted my mother, my father attempted to walk out of the room. In the process of him walking out of the room, he was elbowed by his wife who told him that he had to tell my mother what he came to say. I was not present at the time of his visit, however according to my siblings, it was obvious to them that my father no longer wanted to be in the room with my mother or had anything that he really wanted to say to her. However, my siblings had perceived that he was coerced by his wife to speak to my mother based on his reactions and attitude. Nonetheless, my father turned around and approached my mother. He then, proceeded to tell my mother that he was sorry for treating her the way he did throughout their marriage and asked her to forgive him for everything he put her through. My mother, being the good person that she was, though she was unable to speak and was very weak, shook her head as though she forgave him. When my younger brother, who was present in the room, informed me of the event with my father I couldn't believe what had happened. I was disgusted. How could he ask my mother to forgive him when he didn't mean a word of it. He never asked her to forgive him for his betrayal and abusive behavior in the 33 years of their marriage. Yet, he asked my mother to forgive him because he was coerced to do so by his current wife. I believe that she was feeling guilty for my father's betrayal and she herself was seeking forgiveness through my father.

My mother's second husband never showed up to my sister's house to pay his respects to my dying mother. He did not even have the heart to make it to her wake or her funeral. Even at the point of her dying as she laid on her deathbed he did not care enough to see her prior to her passing. Moreover, he was able to disappoint her one last time by not showing up to her funeral.

Broken

What have I succumbed to.
I'm a wreck.
I am not in denial.
I can barely stand,
nor will I pretend
or fake a smile.

Broken feelings,
never healing,
shattered trust,
I will not forget
the mistakes of my past
that I was unable to correct.

I'm feeling down and worthless,
because of the things that were said
and promises that were made
that burden my soul.
However, the truth will unfold
and memories of it will fade.

THE NEWS

My mother died on February 20th, 2018. I was lying in bed unable to sleep when my cell phone suddenly rang. It was 2:47 in the morning when I got the dreadful call. My older sister called to inform me that the nurse recommended that we all come to the house to say our final good-byes to our mother. The nurse did not expect my mother to live more than an hour or so. As I was taking in the news I struggled to get up. The moment had arrived and I was trying to process it. I thought I had prepared myself for this moment. But, I was shocked and confused. Every thought went blank and I didn't know how to react. Minutes passed which seemed like hours, exactly 5 minutes, and I still remained in bed. Tears were rolling out of my eyes when I received another phone call. It was my sister calling, to inform me that my mother had just passed away in her sleep. I got out of bed and walked around the house, I must have walked around the house in the dark at least three times before I finally sat down on my chair. I remained in my seat for the latter part of two hours thinking the whole time that I had just lost my mother, and wondering what was I going to do without her. Where was I going to go during Mother's Day or the holidays? So many thoughts came to mind. After a while I finally came to terms with losing my mother. Life without her looked gloomy. Ever since her passing, she has been in my thoughts every moment of every day.

As I Close My Eyes

As I close my eyes
I think of you
and of those precious moments
that I shared with you
that I 'll never forget.
I don't want to wake up
from this painful nightmare
That I wish to erase
because you are not by my side.

When I open my eyes
and I return to reality
I try not to cry
as I think of you.
However, when I realize
that you are no longer here
sometimes I cry
when I open my eyes
and I think of you.

With every opening
and closing of my eyes
I think of the unforgettable moments
that together we shared
that someday I hope to enjoy
as I pass and go on to heaven
when I am again by your side.
Wait for me!!!'

THE WAKE

My mother's wake was at the funeral home. There family, friends and loved ones gathered to pay my mother their final respect. Her coffin was surrounded by flowers and inside of it lay my mother. She was dressed in white and her face was covered in make-up just the way she liked it. Everyone walked up to the coffin and shared a private moment with my mother. Many cried as they said their final good-bye to my mother and gave their condolescens to the family. When I walked up to to the coffin to see my mother I too was heartbroken and was barely holding in my tears. However, my 4 year old granddaughter, whom I was holding in my arms, noticed that I was sad. She hugged me tight and asked me if I was sad because my mother was dead. She said that she was sad too because she loved her as well. My heart was shattered upon hearing her comments and tears began to trickle down the corners of my eyes. She said, "abuelo don't cry, I love you too." I made every effort to stop her from watching me cry and told her that I was Ok. I told her that everything was Ok because my mother was with God now. My granddaughter responded yes abuelo your mother is with God now.

A short religious service was conducted by the catholic priest when everyone had settled down and finished paying their respect to my mother. After the service we thanked everyone for attending the service and for being part of my mother's life and welcomed everyone to share their experience, grief and support. Many people took advantage of having been given the opportunity to express their love and admiration for my mother and our family. They shared events and stories in which my mother impacted their lives. As I sat listening to everyone I was overwhelmed as to how much my mother was loved. It was truly a great honor and joy to be able to hear the stories of how my mother made a difference in so many lives. Throughout the wake fotos and videos of my mother were shown for everyone to see. They were fotos of my mother with her children, family, friends and loved ones. They were precious moments frozen in time that we all shared with our mother. Though the pictures and videos illustrated images frozen in time that we shared with my mother they were more than that. In fact, in a way they were telling everyone that they needed to hold on to the memories we all shared with my mother so, that she can continue to be in our hearts even if they were images frozen in time.

Images of You

Images of you,
Frozen in time
brighten my day
and puts into words
these feelings of mine.

Images of you,
In every place,
In my heart,
and in my mind
of beautiful memories
together we made
that I will always embrace.

Images of you,
Gives me something to talk about.
They put a smile on my face
As your soul reaches out
And fills the empty space
Of this Heart of mine.

Though you past away
It is no dismay
When I see images of you
I am kindly reminded
that you are in heaven
In God's Special place.

MY MOTHER'S FUNERAL

My mothers burial took place at a cementary belonging to the funeral home. It began with a brief private viewing. At the funeral home the immediate family members and loved ones were given the opportunity to spend some private time with our mother prior to closing the casket and taking her to the burial site were she would be buried. It was at the funeral home where we saw our mother for the last time. Upon the conclusion of everyone's private viewing our mother was placed in a hearst to be taken to the burial site. The burial site was at a nearby cementary belonging to the funeral home, a short driving distance from the funeral home. We all got in our vehicles and followed the hearst to the burial site.

At the cementary we were able to officially say our final good-bye to our mother, whom we loved and had just lost, prior to being buried. We began our farewell with a religious ceremony conducted by the catholic priest. Together, we prayed for our mother and her soul. Prior to our mother being lowered 6 feet into the ground family and friends all placed a rose on top of my mothers coffin as a symbol of our love which transcends death and will continue to blossom in our hearts as long as we are alive. As she was being lowered many of us present started to cry. It was the moment of realization that from this point on we would no longer be able to see our mother, it struck us like a slap in the face, our mother was dead and now we only had the memories of her to keep us going.

Memories

Precious moments,
together we shared,
will never depart
My grieving heart.

Memories of you,
deep inside my heart,
keeps me from falling
Terribly apart.
Memories we shared,
soothes my pain
when I am weary
and brightens my day.

Memories of your life,
preserves ties that bind,
will never be forgotten,
they bring peace of mind.
Memories of you,
showering me with love
from heaven above,
will forever go on.

AFTER THE FUNERAL

Between the crying and the condolences everyone had forgotten that there is a bright side to everything. My mother was finally resting in peace and no longer suffered from the terrible disease that kept her in agony. In addition, I knew that she no longer had to deal with the dissapointments and desilusionments she encountered throughout her life because of the men she married that actually contributed to her death. Nonetheless, she was no longer alone. God had called for her and was awaiting for her with opened arms, and she had to go. God the son had stood by her bedside the entire time awaiting to walk with her hand in hand through the gates of heaven, where God, the father, was waiting for her arrival. Being a man of faith, I knew the best for our mother had yet to come. She had just entered the gates of heaven and her body no longer was weak and filled with illness. She was in paradise with Christ our Lord and now had a glorious body free of sin. I know she is more alive now than ever because her spirit lives for ever.

I understand that coping with the loss of a loved one can bring up all sorts of emotions, especially at the funeral. I also understand that everyone has their unique way of coping with their loss. However, we cannot disregard the fact that how we mourn relates to our understanding that death comes to everyone and that life continues for those of us left behind. As for our family, after the funeral service we invited our family and friends to gather at my sister's house for a funeral reception with a meal and refreshments. It was something our mother would have wanted for us to do. She loved being around family and friends. She would have not wanted us to mourn her death. Instead, she would have wanted us to celebrate her dlife because, as she would put it, life goes on even after the death of a loved one.

Everyone who gathered at my sister's house was able to open up and share even more wonderful memories of my mother with all of those present. During this time many of the stories told made us laugh and filled us with joy. They definitely eliminated the somber mood of the funeral and reminded us of what our mother meant to all of us and that a little humor is the best way to mourn. We were also able to break bread together with everyone present. A meal which my aunt, sisters and cousins cooked. While they were cooking they were reminded of how my mother loved to cook and of the times that they all cooked together with my mother during the holidays or whenever we all got together at our homes. It was an heartwarming event which reminded us that we need to stay in touch and continue to get together during the holidays, a tradition that our mother loved to do.

Without You

Without you
The sun does not shine
Its light so bright,
nor does it set
on this heart of mine.

Without you
my heart is filled with sadness
that won't go away,
because time can't change
how I feel today.

As I grieve day and night,
my burden soul rages
against the fading light,
that once shined bright,
and gave me sight.

Shine through the darkness
of my broken heart,
and turn my loss and sorrow
with your smile so bright,
into the joy of life.

Although you are gone,
memories of you
lift my anguished soul,
and gives me the courage
to live for tomorrow.

DOMESTIC VIOLENCE

Domestic violence and abuse do not discriminate. It can happen to anyone. It can happen in the form of psychological abuse, whereas the victim is abused verbally and emotionally, or in the form of physical abuse whereas the abusers threatens to hurt or hurts the victims or the loved ones around the victim. No one should live in fear of being victimized by an abuser. Although, men are also victims of abuse, women are more commonly victimized. According to a report released by the Center for Disease Control and Prevention more than half of the killings of American women in the United States die at the hands of their intimate partner. The report also brought to surface that nearly three women, whom are victimized, are murdered everyday die by the person they trusted the most, their curent partner.

My mother was a victim of abusive relationships. She was victimized by the men she loved. Unfortunately, both of the men whom she married were abusers. Both of them attempted to control her by using, fear, guilt, and intimidation. Why she sometimes overlooked the problem and why she did not reach out for help in an attempt to leave the tumultuous relationships in which she found herself astonishes me. She should have never endured such pain. Nonetheless, she did not deserve to be victimized. No one, absolutely no one, deserves to be treated as they were less than human.

My father verbally and emotionally abused my mother. He wore her down since the beginning of their relationship by playing with her emotions. He kept her under his thumb by exploiting the fact that she loved him and was willing to do anything for him. He victimized her by devaluing and disrespecting her to the point that she felt worthless. In addition, he belittled her by having an enormous amount of affairs throughout their marriage and by reminding her of the fact that she did not contribute to their marriage financially. He humiliated her at every possible occasion and did not concern himself with whom he hurt along the way.

My mother's second husband abused my mother physically and emotionally. He too played with my mother's emotions in order to wear her down since the beginning of their relationship. He tried to gain control over my mother by blaming her for his actions. He claimed that his actions were based on the love he felt for her and blamed their fights and every problem they had on her. He made her believe that she had slowly destroyed their marriage based on the fact that she would always take the side of my younger siblings whenever he had a confrontation with any of them. He victimized her by threatening her physically and by threatening to hurt my younger siblings. Though, she never made it known to any of us that he had threaten to hurt her and my younger siblings, it was obvious that he was able to manipulate her. Her behavior at times and her her attitude whenever he was around appeared as though she feared what he could do. The fact, that he had already attempted to kill her earlier during their marriage coupled with the fact that she forgave him gave him more control over her. The problem was clear, however when questioned she would deny any wrong doing or abuse.

My mother's physical and emotional abusive relationships had psychological consequences that lead to her anxiety, high blood pressure, depression and diabetes. Chances are that her unhealthy relationships all contributed to her poor health and were major contributors to her death. I am certain that my mother lived a frightening and confusing life which may have been difficult for others to comprehend. Many of you may ask yourselves, as I have asked myself, Why did she allow herself to be in such an unhealthy relationship for so many years? The thought of it just breaks my heart. Perhaps, it was because of her never ending love for her husbands, the fear she felt for herself or her children, shame of failing in her marriages, or the fact that she may have felt unworthy, is something we will never know. I understand her motive behind not leaving my father. However I often wondered, If sacrificing herself for us was worth dying for. Maybe, her life would have been different had she not sacrificied herself for us. Who knows maybe she would be alive today if she had left my father when she was still young. Perhaps, if she had not lost her sense of self-worth and believed in herself the possibility of her finding a man, who would have married her and raised her children as his own would have resulted in her living a healthier life. If only her thoughts of leaving my father earlier in life could have been a reality, maybe she could have been blessed with a healthier lifestyle and would be alive today. I definitely would have preferred that she would still be alive and healthy. Enjoying life to her fullest even if it meant that I would have been raised by another man who was not my father. I know it is a little harsh but, the fact remains that my father did not have a major role in my life, mainly because he was absent physically and emotionally during my upbringing.

To make matters clear, I have written about my mother's story not because I am being resentful toward my father, whom I love regardless of the past, but in hope that through her story women, who are in a similar situation, find the strength to get out of their abusive relationship before it is too late. First, I urge them to believe that they don't deserve to be a victiom of abuse, and that they can survive and achieve happiness without their abusive partner. Subsequently, I urge everyone who may be a victim of abuse looking to improve their life, to reachout to someone for help. Let someone know your situation, because no one really knows what is taking place behind closed doors, but the victims themselves. Keep in mind that as long as you remain silent no one will hear your plea for help. Understand that you deserve to be happy. Moreover, you need to realize that you don't deserve to be abused by anyone. Lastly, you need to love yourself and not allow anyone to mistreat you. Let people see you for the beautiful person that you are and love you how you deserve to be loved.

A Victim of Violence

She was the victim of a relationship
filled with promises of love,
that turned into terror.
It caused her pain and anguish
which destroyed her spirit
and became her undoing.

At home she felt imprisoned,
humiliated and destroyed
by force and humiliation.
The tools of intimidation
destroyed her spirit and heart
until she fell apart.

She lost her identity,
Spirit and hopes
due to a relationship
where degradation
filled her body with bruises
which she did not deserve.

Her death was the consequence
of physical and emotional acts of violence
of a relationship she could not escape,
where the abuse she tried to hide
in order to protect her home
to her grave the secret she would take.

REFERENCE

www.theatlantic.com/health/archive/2017/07/homicides-women/534306/

www.ingramcontent.com/pod-product-compliance
Lightning Source LLC
Chambersburg PA
CBHW021449070526
44577CB00002B/318